THE LAST WAR HORSES

Contents

World War I	2	Winning the war	18
Cavalry	4	Remembering war horses	20
Working horses	6	Glossary and index	21
Life for a war horse	14	Horses in World War I	22

Written by Charlotte Guillain

Collins

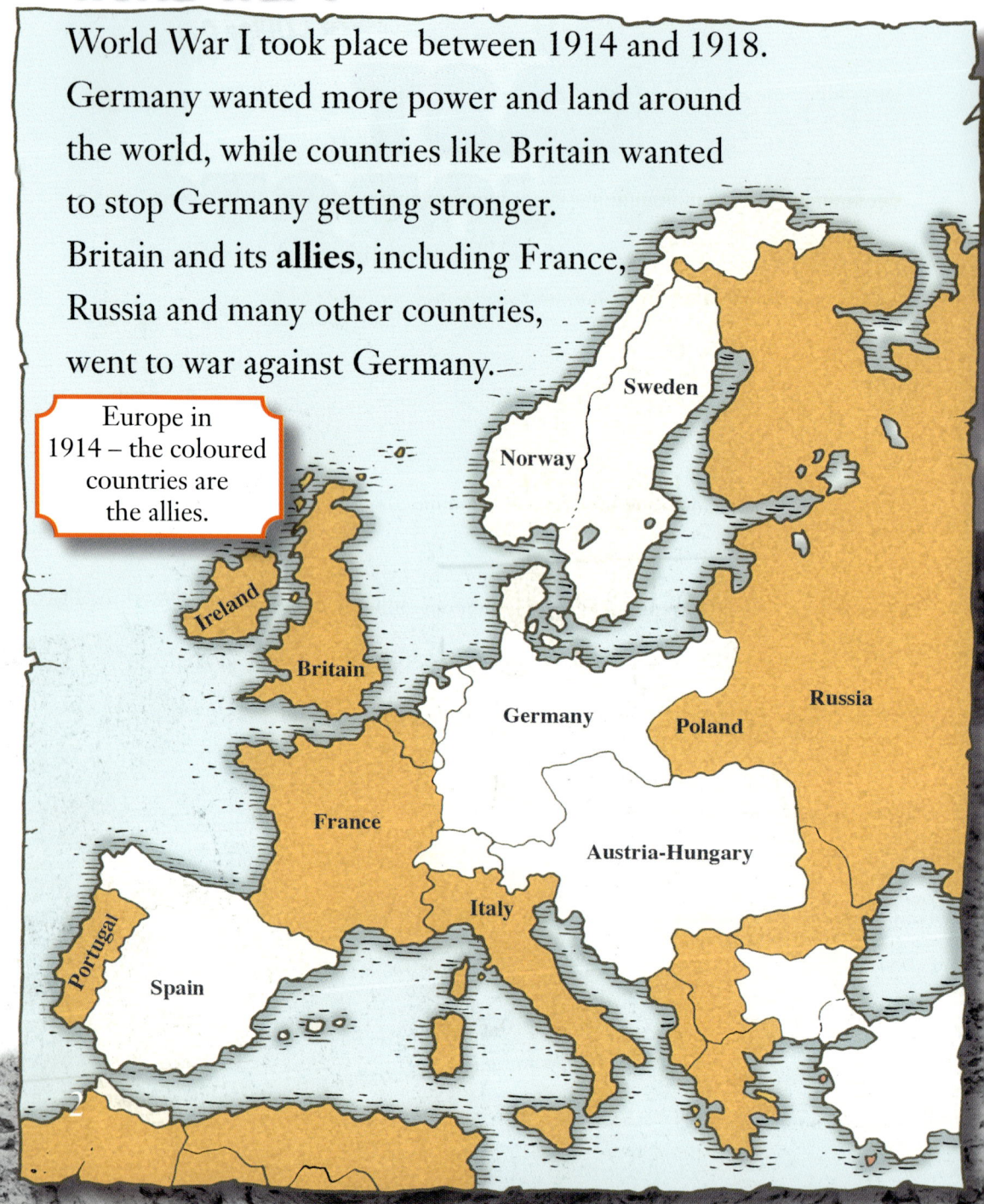

World War I

World War I took place between 1914 and 1918. Germany wanted more power and land around the world, while countries like Britain wanted to stop Germany getting stronger. Britain and its **allies**, including France, Russia and many other countries, went to war against Germany.

Europe in 1914 – the coloured countries are the allies.

Horses helped in different ways during the war.

Cavalry

Before World War I, **cavalry** horses were used in wars. Cavalry horses went into battle carrying soldiers with weapons.

soldiers riding horses into battle at the end of the 19th century

Armies still used cavalry horses at the start of World War I. But many stopped because new machine guns and barbed wire on the battlefield quickly killed many horses.

Barbed wire helped keep soldiers safe in the trenches, but killed many horses.

Working horses

Horses worked in the war zone in other ways. They brought supplies of food and equipment to soldiers at the **front**.

Horses could pull carts over rough and muddy ground where vehicles got stuck. They could also move supplies when railway lines had been bombed.

Large horses took huge guns on carts to the battlefield. The horses had to pull heavy loads over long distances.

But as the war went on, bigger guns were made. Tractors and other vehicles were needed to pull these large weapons.

Tractors could pull heavier weapons than horses but they sometimes got stuck in the mud.

When armies wanted information about enemy positions, they would send spies on horses. They could move quickly and quietly behind enemy lines.

Soldiers also rode horses to carry messages to and from the front.

Millions of soldiers were killed and hurt on the battlefield. Horses pulled carts that worked as ambulances, taking injured men to **field hospitals**.

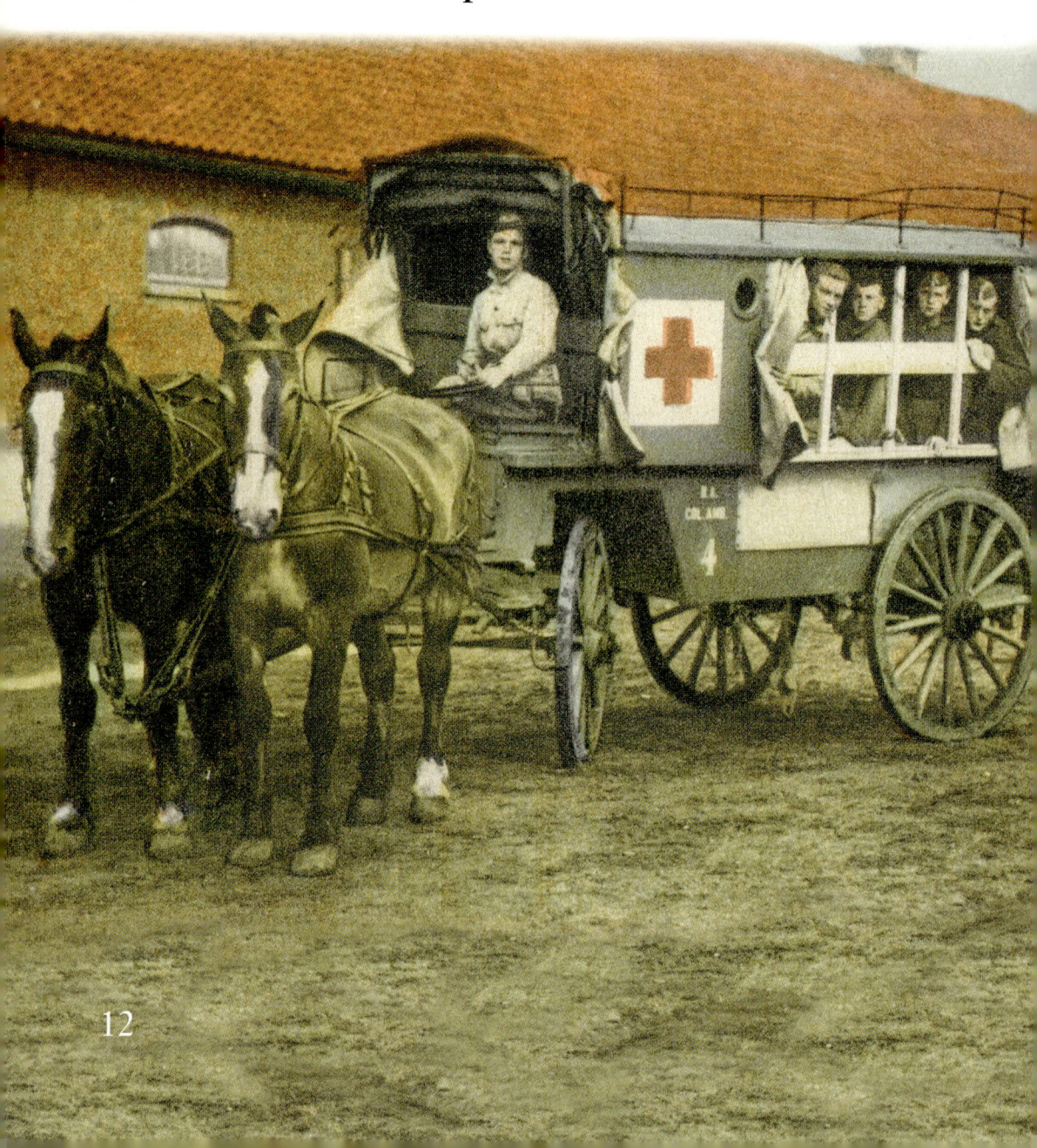

Vets looked after about two and a half million injured horses in **veterinary** hospitals. It was important for the horses to get well so they could return to work.

a vet treating an injured horse during World War I

Life for a war horse

Horses lived in terrible conditions during World War I. They often worked until they dropped and there was little food or proper shelter.

These horses are being fed and rested, but many worked until they dropped.

The battlefield was terrifying for horses. There were loud explosions all around them. Both sides used gas attacks during the war, which affected horses' breathing and burnt their skin.

a horse and soldier wearing gas masks

Many horses became ill because of the stress of hard work or disease. Millions of them died.

The horses also caused problems for soldiers. Tonnes of food had to be transported to feed the animals. The horses' **manure** helped to spread disease among the men.

Winning the war

Towards the end of the war, Britain and its allies stopped the supply of new horses getting through to the German army. This was one reason why the war ended, because Germany could not keep fighting without horses.

a parade celebrating the end of the war in London, 1919

World War I marked the end of horses being used in major wars. Machinery, such as tanks, replaced the need for horses.

Vehicles travelled more quickly over the battlefield than horses.

Remembering war horses

As many as eight million horses died during World War I. Today, people remember the animals that were killed during the war with special **memorials** and statues.

The story of the war horses' terrible experience is still told in books and films today.

This war memorial in France shows a soldier caring for his wounded horse.

Glossary

allies   people or countries who help each other

cavalry   soldiers on horseback

field hospitals   makeshift hospitals set up near a battlefield

front   the place where fighting takes place

manure   animal poo

memorials   something made to remember things

veterinary   to do with helping sick or injured animals

Index

barbed wire 5

battlefield 5, 8, 12, 15

Britain 2, 18

France 2

Germany 2, 18

machine guns 5

railway lines 7

Russia 2

tractors 9

weapons 9

World War I 2, 14, 19, 20

Horses in World War I

Horses were used on spy missions.

Cavalry horses went into battle.

Horses carried supplies of food.

Horses carried large guns.

Horses carried equipment.

Horses pulled ambulance carriages.

🐾 Ideas for reading 🐾

Written by Gillian Howell
Primary Literacy Consultant

Learning objectives: *(reading objectives correspond with Turquoise band; all other objectives correspond with Sapphire band)* read independently and with increasing fluency longer and less familiar texts; know how to tackle unfamiliar words that are not completely decodable; make notes on and use evidence from across a text to explain events or ideas

Curriculum links: History, Citizenship

Interest words: soldiers, battlefield, cavalry, Germany, allies, weapons, machine, supplies, equipment, vehicles, positions, spies, ambulances, veterinary, explosions

Resources: pens, paper, whiteboard, internet

Word count: 486

Getting started

- Read the title together and discuss the cover photo. Ask the children to guess what the book might be about and what the title might mean.
- Turn to the back cover and read the blurb together. Remind the children to look for words within words to help them read difficult vocabulary, e.g. *sold* in *soldiers*, *battle* and *field* in *battlefield*.
- Ask the children what they already know about World War I, and what sort of work they think working horses would do. Note their responses on the whiteboard.

Reading and responding

- Ask the children to read the book aloud quietly. Ask them to make a note of one piece of information that is new to them in each chapter.
- On p2, ask the children to find the countries mentioned in the text on the map. Ask them to find the glossary and read the entry for allies. Remind them to use the glossary as they read to help them understand the words in bold.
- Intervene occasionally as the children read to check they understand the text, e.g. on p9, ask why tractors and other vehicles were needed instead of horses.